LIFE THROUGH A LENS

The Journal of a Young Poetess

LIFE THROUGH A LENS

The Journal of a Young Poetess

By

Khushi Jain

Worldwide Published by

Pendown Press

PENDOWN PRESS

An ISO 9001 & ISO 14001 Certified Co.,

Regd. Office: 2525/193, 1st Floor, Onkar Nagar-A,
Tri Nagar, Delhi-110035
Ph.: 09350849407, 09312235086
E-mail: info@pendownpress.com
Branch Office: 1A/2A, 20, Hari Sadan, Ansari Road,
Daryaganj, New Delhi-110002
Ph.: 011-45794768
Website: PendownPress.com

First Edition: 2020

ISBN: 978-93-90116-52-2

CONTENTS

TEENS

DEDICATION

I dedicate this book firstly to God, as without His blessings, I could not have done anything in my life, be it book writing or any other accomplishments, that are worth mentioning. I also dedicate it to my family and teachers, for without their patience, understanding, support and above all love, the completion of this work could not have been possible. Lastly, to my amazing friends, for without whom I might not have had an interesting life as I do.

PREFACE

The life of a teenager is like a roller coaster ride from from school to college, from friends to relationships, to family. There is surely a party going on inside teenager's head, thinking about what to do, what not to, and what would be the consequences of a particular action. It's too confusing, but the most precious and enjoyable moments that we teenagers had, or we are having, are during our childhood. This book is like a sneak peek into the life and thoughts of a teenaged girl, the teenager me.

Hi! I am Khushi, a 15-year-old from New Delhi. First of all, Congratulations! You have just picked up a series of laughter, enjoyment, fun, and yes some memoirs of sweet moments for you. So, sit back and get ready. No matter in what age group bracket you are, this book will prove to be irresistibly exciting for you. This book is like your diary, the memories of all the feelings, emotions that you experienced in your childhood or teenage, they are all here. This is like living through the lens of a teenaged girl.

As the book graduates, things change—me being a child to a tween, and then a teen. This book has a very fun-loving kind of theme, which not only includes fun topics like teen crushes or Parenting Styles, but also a teen's views on ideas like security for girls or climate change.

In today's world, where we are surrounded by all kinds of digital entertainment and our super busy life, it's important for us not to forget the essence of our feelings and expressions. Let me guarantee you, this book would take you all back in your memory lane .Let's begin the journey. So, sit back and Enjoy!

FOREWORD

I have pleasure in writing this foreword for "The Journal of a Young Poetess" – a collection of poems by Khushi Jain.

Khushi is a girl of much talent and interest and has a vivacious personality. Her poems reflect her thinking on issues that affect young growing teenagers–from their happiness to their concerns, from their influences in daily life to their love for nature.

Khushi belongs to Generation Y and the future belongs to this generation–who must face the challenge of Climate change and Media onslaught!

I wish her all success and I 'm sure her poetry will go a long way in bringing change to the world as a young change maker.

Dr. (Mrs.) Jyoti Bose

Director,
Springdales School
Benito Juarez Marg,
DhaulaKuan, New Delhi-21

CHILDHOOD

1.

I DREAM OF A WORLD FREE OF RACIAL HATRED AND BIAS

I was born in Cape Town,
As a tiny girl I wished to become
a queen with a crown

With my loved ones by my side,
None of my dreams died

Life Through a Lens

Until the time of 1948,
Where humanity met a tragic fate

Grim became the days grim became
the nights, there was racial discrimination
between blacks and whites

My family was arrested,
Our patience and tolerance level were tested

My house and spirits were all shattered,
My dream of becoming queen was hammered

I was kept in concentration camp,
No longer living with love and happiness
I was now in a room with a lamp

Protests, fights and firing what not,
Nothing of which in my childhood I was taught

People were divided in blacks and whites,
Each one of us wanted to get South Africa
out of this plight

Freedom! Freedom! all cried,
They wanted to abolish "Apartheid[1]"

There was a fierce man who then came,
Madiba was his glorious name

He fought with all his might,
Prison was his home for 9855 nights

He became a model for those who had to fight,
And "sparks[2]" who were ready to ignite

I still hold memory of all that we had to suffer,
But this struggle sure made us tougher.

---

1. **Aparthied:** The struggle for equal rights for blacks and whites in South Africa
2. **Sparks:** Those who wanted to be a part of the struggle but didn't know how

2.

TEA OR COFFEE

Everyone loves tea,
It's like every housewife's fee

It is sweet,
Just like a small treat

In colour it is brown!
A perfect taste can save you a frown

It's nice, but in old age makes
you pay the price

It can be replaced by coffee,
Which can be made with caramel or toffee

Made from beans,
and loved by teens

So, choose out of these two,
I have given you the clue

3.

THE ROAD TO A SAFER FUTURE

A safe future is different for you and me,
For the old man wearing baggy clothes
and sitting under the tree,

For the little girl who is working at home
because she cannot pay the school fee,

For the man selling Bread Pakora[1] with morning tea,
It is all different for you and me,

We need to imbibe Aristotle's virtues
Patience, humility, discipline
and ambition is what we need to pursue

The steps to a safer future are on the highway
which is narrow but opportunities wide,
But, you don't be like the hare.

Go slow and steady,
For hardships and difficulties stay all ready.

***

Now a common road of saving the nature
which everyone has to cross,
Is because nature has suffered immense loss.

Today's condition is mankind's mistake,
It has put many lives on stake.

A safe future has become a question mark,
which has hanged mother nature's dream in the dark.

So, to awaken the dreams and secure our lives
we have to take steps and cross stages,
To preserve mankind for ages.

***

It's time to change the thought and recall
the teaching that Mohandas Karamchand Gandhi taught,

Thoughts change by awareness,
This is where the second step comes to harness.

Second step is to be and make people 'AWARE'
So that you and the people around you take care.

Awareness can help us prepare
As without it future can be a nightmare

The third step is to 'ANALYSE' to know
The problem is very essential
As this would tell us where to use our potential

For instance, POLLUTION,
Which seriously needs planning and its EXECUTION.

Controlled Pollution Means Curbing Deaths
Beautiful Sunrise and Sunset and Unobstructed Breaths

Let's move back to nature for a secure future

because when the nature is happy
all the people will be happy

The current scenario brings a thought,
World War 3 with nature has to be fought.

---

1.   **Bread Pakora:** An Indian Snack

4.

MOTHER EARTH

We have the power to save our earth,
She is the one who gave value of our birth

She is kind,
It is what we need to mind

Since posterity she has just given,
There hasn't been an instant
where she has taken

The new generation is trying to keep
the world clean,
Too see the world like that it is keen

So, let us make people aware,
It's time people take care

The clock is ticking,
THINK! What sides are we picking?

☺☺☺

5.

SOUTH AFRICA'S SIGHT

Gloomy were the days gloomy were the nights.
There was racial discrimination
between blacks and whites.

Each one fought with all his might.
The fight got the blacks equal rights.

Nelson Mandela fought with all his might,
letting go all his fright.

Cry and sadness is what all that comes with fight.

Finally, Mr. Mandela came
as a messenger of peace
And slavery came to cease

He ushered a new dawn and era

Happy are the days and happy are the nights
This is the new South Africa's sight

6.

PHONE

Everyone loves the phone,
It can be compared to an ice-cream cone

From Instagram to WhatsApp,
All of us love the crap

iPhone or Samsung "anything"
qualifies to be the best,
and when you have it you forget the rest

Life Through a Lens

It makes you happy,
now kids can have it when
they are in their nappy.

It is good, and catchy,
Thieves around it get snatchy

Everyone loves the phone,
But all repercussions must be known

It gets you all busy and occupied,
for getting it you must have cried.

But remember it gets distraction,
and only momentary satisfaction

It spoils your eyes,
later everyone cries

We can use it for other things to,
Like to know how to get rid of the flu

So much at your fingertips
without having to roam,
Everyone loves the phone

Studies can also be helped,
Or can capture pictures when you wed.

Google maps helps you find the way,
PayTM helps you pay

Phone

You can get food in a click,
Or get an appointment when you are sick

It can be good or bad,
Be cautious when you get it
from your mom or dad

You get excited hearing the ringtone
Everyone loves the phone

7.

STUDIES

These are boring at times,
We just wait for the school bell to chime

History, geography, Hindi are tiring,
But it's interesting to know where was the firing.

They help a lot,
When we are properly taught

We should like them,
They give us knowledge,
Which you would gain even after college

They seem to be bad,
But that's an illusion ask your dad

They are the entertainment in school life,
Better than growing up & fighting with your wife.

They can be interesting,
you can do them while resting.

So, have fun
Until you are all done.

8.

SLEEP

Babies don't like to sleep,
When forced they like to weep

But we love sleeping,
It's definitely better than weeping

At least you dream,
Seeing a nightmare scream

Sleep

It's the best time of the day,
With your pillow and blanket
you are happy and gay

At times while sleeping you snore,
This is the signal to tell your teachers
that the class is bore

Generally, we sleep in history,
A strict teacher stops it in chemistry

Sleep is an antidote and gives you all the rest,
You wake up all excited Ready and well sighted!

Sleep enough,
Or your day would be tough

Sleeping undisturbed is nice,
Don't snooze your alarm
or you would have to pay the price

TWEENS

1.

HAPPY BIRTHDAY TO YOU!

The day has come when our principal was born,
To bring about the spur of change
in each Springdalian ever born

As everyone of us in this world she came,
Through a lot of hard work, she earned the fame

An icon of perfection!
She inspires us to chart the right direction

When we win a competition, her smile has no end,
'more than a feared principal she is a friend

A graduate in sociology,
Her list of awards is even longer
than Indian mythology

Life Through a Lens

Her idea of unity in diversity,
Sculpts Springdalians into an international identity

She has made such a rich contribution to education,
Her gentle aura and talent make you a disarming
combination

Her qualities and perfection have no comparison,
Another like her is yet to be find mention

Three cheers for her hard work and dedication,
It deserves a grand celebration

On your cake, we wish all your dreams come true,
Ma'am a very happy birthday to you!

2.

IAM THE FUTURE

A child is the future of the family
And I am no different

I work very hard and try
To shine in my family's eye.

I am going to be like a rainbow in the sky.

Life Through a Lens

The school plays its part
Adding from the confidence right from the start

Medical, engineering or law
Later the world would look at me in awe

I want to fulfill my parent's dreams
My followers will soon make my team

Every day the school nurtured me
In future, everyone will see

Love, care, and friendship I imbibed
From my teachers, mother and tribe

Integrity, collaboration and hard work-
are some rules of life

Mastering them is an important part.

As they will fetch you top position in a chart

To all challenges these will be my suture
I am the future.

3.

MATHS

Maths is all around us,
It teaches us where to multiply, divide, minus and plus

Sometimes seems difficult but it is not,
Just do a lot of practice,
Then the battle of numbers can be fought

Algebra seemed like an alien to me,
But it became easy when I saw trigonometry

X,y, a and b are all members of the Maths family,
Together they are like branches of a tree

If not solved they unleash wrath

Making you suffer from its aftermath

Through practice I have become its fan,
Be it solving a question related to sin, cos or tan

Comrades play maths like a game,
Don't be feared by its name

Just treat maths like fun,

You will enjoy it and feel pleasure a ton

4.

SISTERS

They can be a lot of trouble
Wish we could pop them like a bubble.

They are never sweet,
Just like an irritating beat;

They take your stuff
and laugh even when you cough.

Longer gets the wait
Whenever you are getting late.

Sissies usually complain,
Eat up your entire brain.

At the end, sisters are the best.
In bedtimes, cling you to their chest

No wonder! They are god's best gift.
Your moods they certainly uplift

When it comes to sisters
no one likes to miss

5.

FRIENDS

They can change your life
You can find one in your friend,
sister or wife

They can be of different kinds
From a careless one to who easily minds

They can be ones who pick you at 4 AM
Or one who call you hey kiddo! instead of hey m!

Life Through a Lens

They cheer you when you are sad
They find good out of all bad

On your birthday, they come uninvited
Seeing them you get all excited

Being with your friends is being the most cool
They are always by your side

Never missed to make a video when you cried

From helping you
or hideously looking at your crush
Or at the breakup getting you
your favorite extra cold slush

Losing one causes a lot of pain
Life then becomes in vain

6.

PARENTING SYLES

They can be fun
Or always on your head with a gun

They can pamper you
Or with petty things hamper you

God knows how they know when you are wrong
Knowing exactly when to sing your favourite song

Parents are forever your Santa
Or for cheering you up get your favourite Fanta[1]

OMG! They can get fussy too
For wearing a mask to avoid the flu

Pretentiously praising your stupid cards is their skill
Their love can never be listed on a bill

From your first step to your wedding
They always know where your mind is heading

Poking on your phones can be torturous
The look after a D grade is monstrous

It doesn't matter how much you fight
They are your parents and they would always be right

☺☺☺

---

1. Fanta: A soft drink

7.

FOOD

Everyone loves junk food
It never fails to lift your mood

From pizza to French fries
It makes you feel joyous and totally satisfies
(is perfect when a cry could not convince me)

Coca Cola is like the icing on the cake
If you don't like it have a milkshake

Ice cream at the last is just the best
Don't have too much
or you'll have congestion in the chest

Junk food needs exercise
Or your clothes would have to double up their size

You would need a doctor to deal with its stuff
Your new friends could be cold and cough

Healthy food isn't so bad
At least it doesn't make your mom feel bad

On taste, it makes you compromise a bit
But remember it makes you fit

Junk or healthy stay is your choice
Every morsel is meant to rejoice

8.

BOOKS

Books are your best friend
Enjoy enough or you will miss it in the end

From Enid Blyton to Roald Dahl
Books make us feel happy
and take us to a world of our own

Where me and my book can enjoy all alone
I wish books could speak; our conversations
would be years long

We would chat without caring
if anything is going wrong
Books can be as much as we want

Just read it with passion
and not when your parents taut
From the cover page, we decide

Whether it is boring or interesting
Is it worth reading while resting

Potterheads[1] are all around
Another author like J.K. Rowling is yet
to be found

Dan Brown, Agatha Christie and
all writers have something new
Sadly, in your bookshelf you can only fit a few

Books according to me are truly unique
Try to read each one as it will make you feel upbeat

---

1.   Potterheads – People who love Harry Potter

TEENS

1.

BACK TO NATURE

Birds singing and chirping all around,
A golden nightingale is yet to be found

Monkeys are made to dance,
It's time mankind takes a clear stance

We love greenery here and there,
But remember nature demands a lot of care

Posters and campaigns help a little bit,
Mankind's efforts would only make wildlife fit.

Back to Nature

Ivory, horns and bushes are sold,
On the alternative side stories,
of preserving nature are told

We need to awaken
There is a call
If measures are not taken
there could be a catastrophic fall.

Nature makes sacrifices in an enormous amount,
it only has pros and no cons
So, never miss a sight for eyes to feast on

☺☺☺

2.

HAPPINESS

It is not very east to get.
Happiness can get your eyes wet

It can come from anything,
from a bouquet to a ring

It may be for seconds or a long time.
You can find it with every clock chime

You can derive it from books
Or how your mother cooks

Happiness

You can find it in dance
Just give yourself a chance

You can find it in singing
Or when you hear your phone ringing.

The first ring from your favorite person
It makes you joyous beyond mention

Everything suddenly changes
from your mood to your voice tone

Just cheer yourself
When you are sad.

Even on a bad hair day
Chocolate can make you gay

It can change your mood.
Just enjoy life a ton

Happiness is
the golden key to fun.

3.

HOLIDAYS

We all love holidays
Love sitting under the Sun and eating Lays1

We go out with family &have fun
All around the kids run.

Sometimes in the cold away from
the scorching sun's ray

We wait for holidays to come.
A completely excited person we become.

We cherish every instant
Forced to visit our relatives distant

Holidays

Everyone loves holidays from elders to kids
On where to go there are bids.

Food is an important part
Everybody hates the flavoured fart

We ski, hike or trek
Get tired from our toes to neck

The weighing scale seems to crack!
Seeing our weight we can't even have
an unhealthy snack

We can have a relaxing massage
And out of pictures make a collage.

When Holidays end
We begin to plan for how
the next holidays we will spend.

1.　Lays – A company for potato chips

4.

SOCIAL MEDIA ADDICTS

OMG! 800 likes
I got 500, yikes!!

Meet today's social media addicts
At times, better than Wikipedia's bits

Multimedia phone is a definite organ
They know Ola![1] to Guten Morgen[2]

WIFI comes as the breath
No network can freeze them to death

Followers make their day
The camera is the inseparable bae[3]

Each picture bringsFOMO[4]
Duh! Why do you even record a race in slo-mo![5]

Vlogging or Blogging
The discovered feed mania gets their mind clogging

Social media Addicts can be fun
for them 0% battery is scarier than a gun!

---

1. Ola! – Greeting in Spanish
2. Guten Morgen- Greeting in German
3. Bae- Before Anyone Else
4. FOMO- Fear of Missing Out
5. Slo- mo – A way to record a video in slow motion

5.

MY FIRST CRUSH

As I walked into my class
My heart shattered like a glass

my crush!
his name brings a blush

was standing behind the chair,
setting his black hair.

Beside him was my best friend
I pulled her away,
I looked at him and said "hey"

My First Crush

My cheeks became tomatoes again
His one look relieved my busy brain

I turned back and sat on the chair
Pretending indifference, I flipped my hair

In history class I turned to have a look
hiding my gleaming face behind the book

He smiled back
music began to play at the back

I visioned him inching towards my seat
We got up and tangoed to the beat

All of a sudden, the bell rang
And the romance was left to hang

I didn't say bye
As I felt a little shy

On Friendship Day, he gave me a band
Not a pinch of dust I let on it land

That day was the best
I kept hideously looking at him forgetting the rest

We played basketball together,
him being on the team even changed the weather

Any foul was fine
I just wanted him to be mine

One day, a new guy entered the school
I started following HIM like a fool

Ah! Then I realised
My list needs to be revised

6.

WHAT'S IT LIKE TO BE
A MOVIE BUFF!

What is it like to be a movie buff?

You have to see every movie whether
you have cold or cough
Answering movie based questions isn't tough

Life Through a Lens

You never need to guess,
Your knowledge saves you from the mess

You get excited to meet stars
In a hurry you don't spare any driver or car

You never miss any merchandise stars make
Ensure that it isn't fake,

The name of the song is enough
to guess the movie name
You laugh even when the jokes are lame

Movie buffing is full of adventure
Those three hours are like a whole new venture

7.

OH! WHY DO YOU EAT WITH YOUR MOUTH OPEN!

Oh! Why do you eat
with your mouth open!

I find it annoying
My feeling, you are toying

Life Through a Lens

I feel pissed off
It's worse than a sneezy cough

I get almost mad
When it stops I am glad

That gurgling sound
To hear it I am bound

It irritates me
When I complain everyone hates me

Vgh! What is this crunch
Just stop this loud munch

Enough with your chomp! chomp!
Beware! I'll turn you into a PomPom

Oh! for lord's sake
This trend I got to break

Please stop eating
with your mouth open

☺☺☺

8.

GIRL ON THE ROADSIDE

Standing on the main road on the pavement
Carefully tracking every movement

Waiting for my mom to pick me up
A bark was enough to scare me up

With each car passing by
I was getting goose bumps

I felt my heart beat
As anyone stared
at me sitting on the car seat

I was scared and I wondered
Was wearing a shirt and shorts a sin?
It was freedom what I wished from a gin

Two boys then passed by on a bike
Battling each stare was warlike

Mom appeared to pick me up
I quickly settled in the car avoiding
any other walk up

Thoughts of rape began to cloud my mind
A solution to this problem
we together need to find